OPTIONS TRADING FOR BEGINNERS

The A-Z Guide to Making a Steady Monthly Income by Trading Options

JORDAN WAYNE

© Copyright 2018 by Jordan Wayne - All rights reserved.

The following book is reproduced below with the goal of providing information that is as accurate and reliable as possible. Regardless, purchasing this book can be seen as consent to the fact that both the publisher and the author of this book are in no way experts on the topics discussed within and that any recommendations or suggestions that are made herein are for entertainment purposes only. Professionals should be consulted as needed prior to undertaking any of the action endorsed herein.

This declaration is deemed fair and valid by both the American Bar Association and the Committee of Publishers Association and is legally binding throughout the United States.

Furthermore, the transmission, duplication or reproduction of any of the following work including specific information will be considered an illegal act irrespective of if it is done electronically or in print. This extends to creating a secondary or tertiary copy of the work or a recorded copy and is only allowed with an expressed written consent from the Publisher. All additional rights reserved.

The information in the following pages is broadly considered to be truthful and accurate account of facts, and as such any inattention, use or misuse of the information in question by the reader will render any resulting actions solely under their purview. There are no scenarios in which the publisher or the original author of this work can be in any fashion deemed liable for any hardship or damages that may befall them after undertaking information described herein.

Additionally, the information in the following pages is intended only for informational purposes and should thus be thought of as universal. As befitting its nature, it is presented without assurance regarding its prolonged validity or interim quality. Trademarks that are mentioned are done without written consent and can in no way be considered an endorsement from the trademark holder.

TABLE OF CONTENTS

Introduction 1

Chapter 1 : Options 101 2

    What are options? 2

    Options in the stock market 3

    The broker 3

    The market maker 4

    The Options Clearing Corporation 5

    Options Industry Council 5

    Why were options such a hit? 6

    Options vs. stocks 6

Chapter 2 : Buying and Selling Options 8

Chapter 3 : Key Influencers on the Prices of Options 12

Chapter 4 : Benefits of Options Trading 16

    Cost efficiency 17

    Less risk 17

    Higher potential returns 18

    Flexibility and versatility 19

Chapter 5 : Shortfalls of Options Trading 20

    Tax 20

    Commissions 21

    Time value decay 21

    Uncertainty of gains 21

    Loss of investment 22

    Regulation 22

    Lower liquidity 22

    Complicated 23

    Leverage 23

Chapter 6 : Types and Styles of Options 24
Calls 25
Puts 25
American style 26
European style 26
Exchange-traded options 26
Over the counter options 27
Option type by underlying asset 27
Option type by expiration 27
Employee stock options 28
Exotic options 28

Chapter 7 : Options Prices and Valuation 29
What are the main influences of the price of an option? 30
Intrinsic value 30
Time value 30
In the money 31
At the money 31
Out of the money 32

Chapter 8 : Roles of Options Exchanges 33
Liquidity 33
Gauging a country's economy 34
Securities pricing 34
Safety of transactions 34
Providing speculation scope 35
Promotes investment culture 35
Continuous market for securities 35
Capital formation 35
Control companies 36
Fiscal and monetary policies 36

Proper canalization of wealth 36

Education purposes 36

Chapter 9 : Roles of the Options Clearing Corporation 37

Clearing services 37

Market data 39

Risk management 40

Chapter 10 : How to Open a Trading Account 43

Scout for options brokers 44

Application 45

Approval 45

Technical analysis 45

Chapter 11 : Placing Your Order 46

Chapter 12 : What Are Options Chains? 49

Basic options chain 50

Options pricer 51

Options strategy chain 51

Chapter 13 : How to Make Trades 52

Decide which direction you think the stock is going to move 53

Predict the changes in stock price—whether high or low 53

Predict the timeframe during which the underlying will move 53

Chapter 14 : Significant Trading Tools 55

Demo account 55

Trading bots 56

OptionsOracle 56

StockFetcher 56

Chapter 15 : Strategies for Options Trading 58

Covered call 58

Married put 59

Bull call spread 59

Bear put spread 60

Protective collar 60

Long straddle 60

Butterfly spread 61

Iron condor 61

Iron butterfly 61

Chapter 16 : Sources of Information 62

Consolidated tapes 63

Pink Sheets 63

Yellow Sheets 63

Nasdaq 64

Blue List 64

Bond Buyer 65

Apps 65

Chapter 17 : Common Mistakes to Be Wary of 67

Buying out of the money call options 67

Giving in to fear and greed 68

Doing poor allocation 68

Having a finite approach 68

Not having an exit plan 68

Being oblivious to market moving events 69

Ignoring consistent profits in favor of home runs 69

Buying naked options without hedging 69

Trying to time legged trades 69

Having a strategy that doesn't match your outlook 70

Choosing an inappropriate date of expiration 70

Not using probability 70

Not having a trading plan 70

Conclusion 72

Introduction

Both beginner and experienced traders seem to agree that trading options is considerably tougher than other types of trading. Many people seem to think that options are risky and that they are only suitable for rich investors. The truth is that mastering options is like mastering anything else: there are rules you must follow. Virtually any investor can use options to expand their portfolio and finally achieve financial freedom. One of the biggest advantages of options is that the earning potential is huge. You can also use options as a hedge. In this era of uncertainties in the financial markets, you have no idea what the future holds. Options can insure your portfolio from market downturns. A trader who wants to start making serious bank should put themselves into the ring and start trading options. Options give you all the tools you'll need to leverage your business and turn even a small capital into big-money business.

Chapter 1

Options 101

What are options?

Options are a financial derivative purchased from an option writer. It is on the option's holder to purchase or sell an underlying security for the agreed amount within a specified timeframe. A call describes the situation where the option's holder can buy the underlying at the strike price, whereas a put describes a situation where an option's holder can sell an underlying at the strike price. In a broad sense, options trading bear a close resemblance to stock trading. A stock trader makes a profit through buying and selling stock at a greater price, and an options trader makes a profit through buying options contracts and selling at a greater price. There are many investment paths that an options trader could take considering that options contracts are based on a wide range of underlying securities. Options can be used to speculate on the price movement of indices, stocks, currencies, commodities, and other tradable financial assets.

Options in the stock market

Buying options takes an approach similar to buying stocks. You basically expect to sell the options at a price greater than what you paid for it. You have to specify the type and number of securities when buying an option contract and then open an order with a broker. If the value of your options goes up, you are in a position to make a profit should you elect to sell them. If you expect the worth of an underlying security to go up, you may buy call options, thus acquiring the right to purchase the underlying security at the strike price. If you anticipate the value of an underlying asset to fall, you may buy put options and acquire the right to sell off the underlying security at the strike price.

There are two ways you may sell your options contracts; first, by putting a sell to close order, and second, by short selling them after opening a short position. Options trading can be quite a complex undertaking. If you're just starting out, you have to scout for a platform with a great reputation and plenty of educational resources. Some of the considerations that influence the most suitable platform include cost, beginner or active trader, research, and education.

The broker

The success or failure of an options trader depends in large measure on the broker they are associated with. You have to select a broker that caters to your specific needs. For instance, if you're a beginner, you have to look for a broker that offers extensive educational resources and assists beginners through their early stage. Options brokers offer trades in common options and other tradable securities, such as stocks, mutual funds, exchange-traded funds, and bonds. An ideal options broker for a beginner-level trader must offer a low minimum and user-friendly platform. This will allow the beginner to adjust accordingly into the right trader's mindset without necessarily making costly mistakes.

A great options broker must have advanced research tools. The trader can select from a wide range of assets, and they should be able to do research so that they can make informed decisions. If you make your decisions based on misinformation and ignorance, it is obviously going to cost you. A great broker must also have superior trading tools. This is important as it helps to execute trades with much ease. Low commissions are important too as they increase the earnings of the trader.

The market maker

The work of market makers is to keep the financial markets efficient by ensuring a certain level of liquidity. They have contracts with various exchanges and they carry out large volumes of transactions. Market makers ensure that the market operates smoothly. They enable traders to buy and sell options even in the absence of public orders to match the required trade.

Market makers maintain an extensive portfolio of different options contracts. They are responsible for the depth and liquidity in the options exchanges. Without market makers, the options trading market would stagnate and traders would have a hard time. Considering the critical role that they play, market makers enjoy various privileges in the industry. The intention of each market maker is to make a two-sided market in the options of various securities. Thus, the market maker can buy from traders or sell to traders at any time. Market makers earn a profit from the price difference, and considering the volatile nature of prices in the trading markets, the earning potential is pretty large. Large corporations seem to be slowly displacing the individuals who previously acted as market makers, as these corporations utilize expensive technology that automates the trading.

The Options Clearing Corporation

This organization is registered as a Derivatives Clearing Organization, and it's regulated by the Commodities Futures Trading Commission. The Options Clearing Corporation provides equity derivatives clearing and central counterparty clearing services. This organization is both the issuer and guarantor for options and futures contracts. It is the biggest financial derivatives clearing organization on the planet. The goal of this organization is to ensure that equity derivative exchanges are stable. The Options Clearing Corporation sees to it that all the requirements of the contracts it clears are met. This organization has held custody to an estimated $100 billion of collateral belonging to clearing members, and billions are transacted every day. The Options Clearing Corporation plays an indispensable function in the financial market, and it draws the largest percentage of its income from charging members. The organization also provides risk-control services. Its clients include professional traders, brokers, dealers, futures merchants, and other securities firms. By guaranteeing that transactions will take place as pledged, it promotes efficiency and orderliness in the derivatives market.

Options Industry Council

The Options Industry Council was created in 1992 by the US options exchanges and the Options Clearing Corporation. Its main function is to educate investors and other parties in the financial sector about the advantages and shortcomings of equity options traded in an exchange. This cooperative is the industry's largest education resource concerning equity options. Some of the large corporations that sponsor the Options Industry Council include the Boston Options Exchange, BATS Options, C2 Options Exchange Inc., the International Securities Exchange, the Chicago Board Options Exchange, Nasdaq Options Market, NASDAQ OMX PHLX, NYSE Arca, NYSE Ames, and the Options Clearing Corporation. The educational resources of the Options Industry Council may be accessed through online classes, podcasts, brochures, and DVDs.

Options are complex products. It's why the Options Industry Council (OIC) conducts hundreds of seminars throughout the year. Additionally, the OIC maintains a website that articulates everything about their educational resources. Most of their content are generated by experienced options industry professionals and then reviewed by compliance and legal entities to ensure that the message comes out as intended. Some of the materials provided at the OIC's website include options basics, trading strategies, advanced concepts, calculators, trading tools, trading data, newsroom, options store, and market quotes.

Why were options such a hit?

The life of a professional trader is vastly different from the life of an ordinary employee. The greatest thing about trading professionally is the level of freedom that it affords you. As an options trader, you're not restrained by a rigid schedule and you can work whenever you please. Studies show that a huge percentage of American workers detest their jobs. Having to wake up and spend your day at a job that sucks your soul is a taxing thing. But here comes an avenue for making money—lots of money—that doesn't require you to go to work! As a trader, you can work in your pajamas, or even while you're on vacation! Options trading took off because they carried the hopes of many people who wanted to escape corporate slavery and get rich while they're at it. Obviously, not everyone who's an options trader gets to earn big sums of money, but that possibility is enough of an incentive.

Options vs. stocks

Both traders and investors share a common goal, i.e., earning profits. Instinctually, they both want to minimize the risk as much as possible and increase their margins of profit. If you're new to the trading scene, you can easily get overwhelmed and make decisions that end up costing you. Both options and stock fall into a similar pattern of earning profits, i.e., buying when the current worth of an asset is small so that you might sell at a profit when the security reaches its intrinsic value. An options trader buys and sells options contracts whereas a stock trader buys and sells stocks. Admittedly, options trading is more complex than stock trading, and for that reason, it requires sharper analytical skills as well as mental stamina. A stock trader will only have to make one significant decision—whether the stock price will go up or down. On the other hand, an options trader will have to make three decisions: the direction that the derivative is heading, how high or low the price changes are, and the time-scope for these changes.

Chapter 2

Buying and Selling Options

If you purchase options, it doesn't necessarily mean that you will purchase the underlying asset. In other words, you have options. For one, you may wait for your options to reach maturity before you trade. When the contract reaches maturity, you might choose to exercise the option, buying or selling at the strike price.

For instance, if you purchase a call at $25 strike price and, at the expiration date, the market price of the stock is $35, you might exercise your option at $25 and earn a $10 profit from every share. You may exercise your call option within the lifetime of the options contract. For instance, you might purchase a call for $25, and thereafter, the price starts oscillating above and below your strike price. This is obviously bound to set off your alarms. If the underlying's price rises to $30, you might be forced to act quickly before the price goes down and thus exercise at $25, earning a profit of $5 per share. Also, you can wait for the option contract to expire. For instance, if you buy a call option at a $25 strike price and the value of the underlying asset stagnates or decreases, you might be forced to wait until the contract expires. Since you haven't taken any action, you will not earn a profit, and the loss you'll incur will be limited to the commissions and the premiums you paid for the options.

An investor will buy a call if they expect the price of the underlying security to go up. Buying a call option permits you to purchase the underlying asset at the strike price before the contract expires, but not many traders see it through. Some of the factors that influence the call options you'll buy include the amount of time you intend to be in the trade, the sum you can spend on buying a call option, and the period you expect the price adjustments to take.

Premium is the sum you pay in order to acquire the option. The premium is affected by several factors; among them are implied volatility, expiration, and type of option. Implied volatility leads to an increased premium. The longer an option will take to expire, the more time there is for the price of the asset to head in the right direction, which necessitates a higher premium. An in the money option will cost more than an out of the money option. Your selection of the strike price and expiration all depends on your assessment of the underlying asset.

Options can also be purchased as a means of insuring against potential losses for an underlying asset. When an options trader pays premium, their expectation is that the value of the security will increase and that they can earn a profit. The options buyer pays for the intrinsic value of an asset and must wait for the extrinsic value in order to make a profit. If the price stagnates, or if the price moves slowly in the right direction, the move is affected by time decay. Implied volatility oscillates up and down according to the supply and demand for options contracts. The nearer the strike price and the stock price are, the more volatile the option will be to adjustments in implied volatility.

When it comes to options trading, mental stability is of utmost importance, but that's not all you'll need. Following are some of the other qualities that you should possess in order to be a successful options trader:

- **Patience.** Look for stocks that are on the lower side of the price and buy their options contracts cheap so that you might sell them for a higher price at a later time. You want to maximize the risk vs. reward scenario. Also, you should be patient enough to wait for the asset to hit the highest possible price so that you can maximize your profit margin.

- **Diversify.** In options trading, there's a potential for earning big; in the same breath, there's a potential for losing big. The intelligent investor/trader is not a chance-taker. Rather, they have a strategy. Desist from putting all your eggs in one basket. Buy calls and puts on several securities in various industries. It is wise to spread out your purchases across the year so that you can create the sense that there's no end to your profits while also shielding yourself against losing streaks, which can easily demoralize you.

- **Minimize your risk.** Aim for the highest profit imaginable while spending just enough. Lower your risk as much as possible. Stay informed on the happenings of the market so that you could make appropriate decisions. If an option drops by 50%, you should consider selling it.

- **Plan.** Don't become the sort of person who trades on a whim. Rashness is likely to lead you into an expensive mistake. When you take your time to plan your trading strategy, you will source together all the relevant resources and your execution of the trade will be perfect.

- **Check your greed.** In options trading, the line between greed and patience is blurred. For instance, if a stock tends to oscillate and then it suddenly runs all the way up, you might be tempted to think that it will go up even further, but it might be better to just close the trade and feast on your profits.

- **Don't overpay.** There are many brokers offering great deals. Don't rush into setting up an account with the first broker that you read about. Always have an idea of what you're willing to pay, and take a pass on options whose premiums are more than you're prepared to give.

- **Power of leverage.** Find options whose value will increase by a great percentage.

Chapter 3

Key Influencers on the Prices of Options

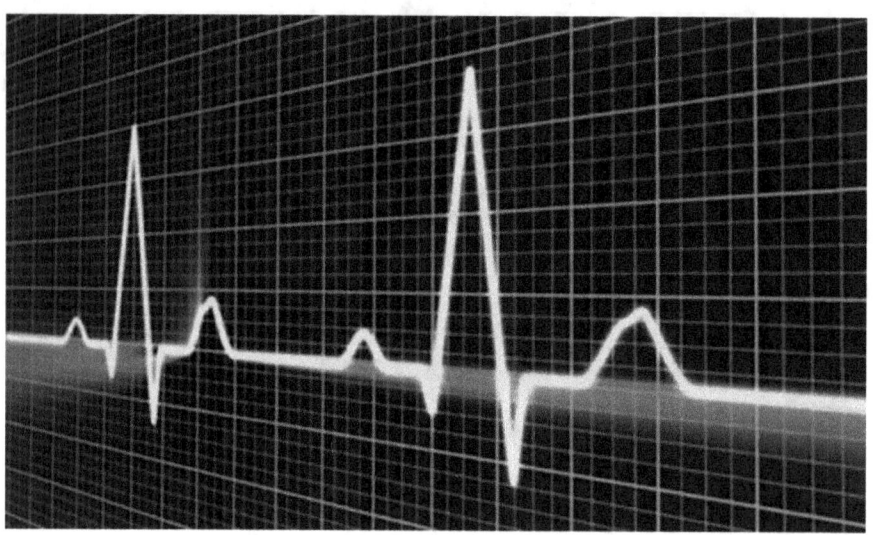

There are many options strategies, but they all arise from two basic options: the call and the put. The put grants the holder the right to sell the underlying security at the strike price before the contract expires. If the stock price is greater than the strike price when the contract expires, the contract is considered to have zero value and would thus expire worthless. A call entitles the holder to buy the underlying at the strike price before the contract expires. If the strike price is greater than the stock price at the date of expiration, then the option expires as worthless.

In both puts and calls, the market maker or investor receives a premium. The premium is the fee of acquiring an option. Here are some of the actors that affect the price of an option:

- **Probability.** The chance that an option will end up in the money is the main aspect influencing an option's worth. The closer the probability that the underlying asset will end up in the money gets to 100%, the greater the worth of the option becomes; the further away the probability that the underlying asset will finish in the money gets from 100%, the lower the value of the option. As a trader, you have to sharpen your analytical skills and determine whether an option is worthy of the premium it demands.

- **Stock price.** If you want to acquire an option that entitles you to buy a stock at $50 per share, the premium would be affected by how close the stock price is to the $50, i.e., you would pay more if the stock was trading at $45 as opposed to $40. The higher the stock price, the higher the premium of call options. In the same vein, the lower the stock price, the higher the premium of put options. If you want to sell an underlying at $30, you will pay more for the put option when the strike is at $28 as opposed to $35.

- **Time to expiration.** When there's a lot of time left for the options contract to expire, chances are high that the price of the underlying asset will undergo significant changes. Thus, the premium will be high. On the other hand, as the expiration approaches, the chances of significant change in the price of underlying assets tend to diminish, thus lowering the premium. The date of expiration causes options to have a definitive nature. Thus, if the price of an option seems unbearable, you might consider waiting for the period to expiration to thin out.

- **Volatility.** This is the measure of how swiftly and extensively the price of an underlying asset jumps up and down. Generally, the most profitable options contracts are volatile in nature. The more frequent and extensive the oscillations, the more likely the option's price will go up. Even the slightest change in the estimated volatility can have a large impact on the premium. A shrewd trader should take the time to research the financial securities that are significantly volatile so that they can maximize their earning potential. The price oscillations of an underlying asset in the recent past are used to determine the premium. If the market takes over and the oscillations happen from moment to moment, then you have a case of implied volatility.

- **Interest rates.** It is important to note that rates of interest have a slight effect on the value of an option. When the rates of interest increase, the worth of the call will go up, and the put option will go down. The adjustments in the premiums are triggered by the costs of owning the underlying assets. When a trader acquires an options contract, the extra cash can attract interest. A high interest translates into bigger earnings. For this reason, traders are willing to pay higher premiums to own call options.

- **Dividends.** When a trader fails to receive their dividend, the stock will go down by that amount. A dividends increment causes a rise in the value of both calls and puts.

- **Natural logarithm.** The Black-Scholes calculation of premiums utilizes the natural logarithm. The changes in the price of underlying assets are proportional to the price of the underlying.

- **Normal distribution.** Normal probability distribution is used in the calculation of an options price. In the Black-Scholes model, price movement is understood to be distributed normally. Small movements have high probability, whereas large movements have low probability.

- **News.** It seems that financial news plays a critical role in driving the whole derivatives markets. Although chances of it happening are rare, influential finance journalists could drive an agenda that could trigger oscillations in the price of options contracts. But the real captains of the industry are the brokers and market makers. These people who are in charge of brokerages and market making corporations have the power to influence the course of the derivatives market. When they appear on the news, traders and investors hang on their every word and traders could go on a spree of buying or selling, which obviously affects the value of options.

- **Crowd psychology.** If there's a sector that asks for mental maturity and discipline, it's the derivatives market. You have to have a plan and know when to take actions as opposed to guessing your way around. But people are still people. It's so easy to get distracted by the trends and lose sight of your trading strategy. For instance, if a certain clique of traders reaps sudden profits, everyone runs into their niche in the hope of reaping quick benefits, thus driving the premium of the option up.

Chapter 4

Benefits of Options Trading

Exchange-traded options first began in 1973. Although options have been termed as a risky investment, even a newbie trader can easily master them as long as they are dedicated. But it is critical for one to be informed before they start engaging in options trading, for the simple reason that improper execution can lead to a major loss. In recent times, the popularity of options trading has grown rapidly, and more people are discovering the joys of being an options trader. Here are some of the benefits attached to options trading:

Cost efficiency

The leveraging power of options is great. Thus, a trader may acquire an option position similar to a stock position, but at a significantly lower price. With options trading, it is possible to make great profits without necessarily having large amounts of money. Individuals that operate on a tight budget have found options trading very accommodating. A shrewd trader can employ leverage to increase their trading power without necessarily injecting more capital.

Let's suppose that you had $1000 and wanted to invest in a company whose stock was trading at $20 per share. On the one hand, you could elect to buy the company's stocks and thus acquire 50 shares. If the stock price increases to $25, you would make $5 profit for every share you own, and your total profit would be $250. This is a 25% return on investment! On the other hand, you could purchase call options on the same stock and gain the right to purchase it. Assuming that the call options with a $20 strike price were trading at $2, you could purchase 500 options, which would enable you to purchase 500 shares. Assuming that the stock price increased to $25, you could exercise your option to purchase 500 shares and, upon selling your shares, you'd make a grand total of $2500. This is a staggering 150% return on investment! The greatest appeal of options trading is that it enables traders to execute cost efficient trades even as it widens their earning capacity.

Less risk

Some people are scared of ever getting into the derivatives trading market, lamenting that it is a very risky pursuit, but that's not really the case. Of course, there are instances when options can be risky, yet there are also situations wherein options can actually help you minimize risk. It all comes down to how you utilize them. Options take less financial commitment than equities, and they are also resistant to the negative effects of gap openings.

Options are great for hedging. When a trader purchases stocks, a stop-loss order is activated to shield the position. The stop-loss order terminates trades that go under a price preset by the trader. Let's assume that you buy a stock at $50. You're not planning on losing more than 10% of your investment, so you put a $45 stop order. When the stock price goes below $45, it will become a market order to sell immediately. Many unforeseeable events could work to your disadvantage and cause you to make a loss. For instance, there might be fraud, causing the stock price to pummel all the way down to $20. Thus, you will sell at $20 when the stock opens, incurring a huge loss. The stop-loss order somewhat couldn't help. But if you had bought the put option, you wouldn't have been hit by such a loss. When the market closes, options do not shut down, unlike the stop-loss orders. Options are quite reliable as they insure your assets both day and night. For this reason, many investors choose options for hedging purposes. Furthermore, purchasing an in the money call instead of stocks in that scenario would have resulted in a minor loss, since your loss would be limited to the premium that you paid to acquire the options contract and not the entire stock.

Higher potential returns

Options have a huge potential for returns. You can spend less money and earn almost the same profit. Most traders are attracted by the promise of making so much money with considerably less capital. If the right trading strategies are employed, options can give a much better risk vs. reward ratio. Obviously, there are certain risks involved, just as you would expect risks in any type of investment. The riskiest trading strategies are the ones that are speculative in nature. Generally, the higher the potential of earning, the riskier the investment; thus, you can control the level of risk that you're ready to suffer. The wide range of options contracts to purchase makes it far easier to limit risk as opposed to simply buying and selling stock.

Flexibility and versatility

Another benefit of options is the flexibility that they offer. For instance, if your investment approach is to buy and hold, you will simply buy stocks either for the long term or short term. The long-term stocks should appreciate in value over time and the short-term stocks should perform faster for regular dividends. The investment strategy of buying stocks doesn't confer to investors avenues of risk limitation or strategies of increasing their earning potential. As a stock trader, the method of earning a profit is linear, i.e., you either buy stocks that you think will appreciate or short sell stocks that you think will depreciate. But when it comes to options trading, the flexibility and versatility afford an investor many opportunities of earning huge profits as dictated by the prevailing markets. Options can be purchased or sold based on a wide selection of underlying assets. You can speculate on the movement of stock price, commodities, foreign currencies, indices, etc. The challenge is to identify opportunities for profitable trades. Spreads can make your trades more flexible, and they can be applied in hedging positions as well, which is a critical step during uncertain market conditions. A trader can also profit from stagnant markets by utilizing options spreads, an action that is hard to replicate in stock trading.

Chapter 5

Shortfalls of Options Trading

Options have many advantages, but just like any other investment, they have disadvantages too. It is critical for the investor to understand both sides of the coin, the good and the bad, before they commit their resources into options trading. Following are some of the shortfalls of options trading.

Tax

With the exception of extremely rare instances, all your gains are taxed as income. This is the same as taxing your personal income because the tax rates levied upon your gains are just as high. One clever way investors can step around the taxation issue is to utilize their tax-deferred accounts such as the IRA. Sadly, not everyone has ownership of a tax-deferred account. Obviously, the tax can reduce the amount of money you take home, but considering the high earning potential, options are still profitable.

Commissions

In comparison to stock investing, commissions for options are significantly higher. For most active traders, their annual commissions usually exceed 30% of the total amount you invested. In order to guard yourself against paying exorbitant commissions, never sign up with a broker without being clear. Whenever you receive a newsletter, quickly check to see the commission details. Options trades will cost you more in commission for every dollar that you put down. The commissions may even be more for spreads that require you to pay commissions for both its sides. A trader should be careful about the broker that they choose to work with. For instance, if you're a beginner, you should stick to brokers who cater to beginners.

Time value decay

In stock trading, you can purchase long-term stocks that can take decades to mature. But options contracts come with an expiration date. There is nothing that you can do to stop the process of expiring. Also, the option's position relative to the date of expiration affects the premium that you will pay to acquire the option. The more the options get closer to the expiration date, the more the rate of time value decay increases. Therefore, you should keep an eye on your open positions so that your options don't expire worthless.

Uncertainty of gains

Investors try to minimize risk by examining the risk profile graphs. This shows them the projected gains or losses at the next expiration of options contracts. In as much as these graphs are helpful, especially when placing the initial position, they still cannot guarantee you a profit. It can be hard to project the gains from an options trade.

Sometimes, after the expiration of options contracts, the expected gains are not generated. But there are other times when, at the expiration of options contracts, the earnings exceed the projected gains. In that sense, your gains or losses become somewhat uncertain—terrible for individuals who loathe uncertainty.

Loss of investment

The extent of your losses depends in large measure on your investment strategy. If you put together a strategy aimed at the highest possible returns, the risk is considerably higher as well. Options contracts give you the right to buy various underlying assets. During the lifetime of the contract, the underlying's price can depreciate, and at expiration, you would obviously not exercise your option. The good thing is that you only lose the premium; a stock trader would lose their shares.

Regulation

One of the things that bother traders and investors are the regulations imposed by governing bodies. The OCC, Securities and Exchange Commission (SEC), or even the court has the power to impose restrictions on exercising various options. Although it rarely happens, it is still enough of a concern that it can make traders think again before putting down their resources into acquiring options contracts. You should always perform your due diligence over the underlying assets that you intend to take options contracts for. If the assets are at the center of legal battles, you might want to take a pass.

Lower liquidity

A lot of individual stock options don't have much volume. Unless it is one of the most popular stocks or stock indexes, the option you're trading is likely to be low-volume because each stock will have different strike price and expiration. It is important to note that the liquidity issue only becomes a huge factor if the trades are big-money. In the case of a small trader who purchases around 10 options contracts, liquidity is never going to be an issue.

Complicated

It's not beginners alone who can get overwhelmed in the world of options trading. There are professional traders who seem to think that they understand options trading when they clearly don't. In order to understand options trading, you have to dedicate a significant amount of time to studying all the aspects of this field. As a beginner, the worst mistake you can commit is to sign up with a broker that caters to professional traders. You have to look for a broker that caters to beginners so that you could utilize their educational resources. There's so much to learn before anyone could become proficient in options trading.

Leverage

When it comes to options trading, leverage is a double-edged sword. On the one hand, it can minimize the risk surrounding an underlying, and on the other hand, it can affect the performance of the asset's market value. Obviously, when the price of an underlying is affected negatively, it means that your earning potential is constrained. Leverage is most dangerous when you're selling naked options or entering into unlimited-risk strategies. Options trading affords investors many trading tools. The tools can make or break you. It is upon the investor to use these trading tools for their benefit. The biggest step an investor can take for success in options trading is to first acquire the requisite knowledge. Guesswork is bound to get you into major losses.

Chapter 6

Types and Styles of Options

There are various types of options that can be traded, and they can be categorized in a number of ways. Calls and puts are the two main option types. Calls entitle the buyer to buy the underlying asset, whereas puts entitle the buyer into selling the underlying asset. Additionally, options are normally categorized based on whether they are American style or European style. Furthermore, options can be classified based on the method by which they are traded, the cycle of expiration, and the underlying security associated with them.

Calls

Call options grant the holder the right to purchase the underlying. They have an expiration date and, depending on the terms, the holder can purchase before the contract expires. A call is essentially a financial contract between the options writer and the buyer. The holder of the call acquires the right to buy the underlying. The options writer receives payment from the buyer. The contract contains critical details such as the strike price, expiration date, and the underlying assets.

A contract must be based on an underlying asset. For instance, if you bought a call based on shares in company C, then you've purchased the right to buy the shares of company C. The strike price will determine at what price you will buy the underlying asset. If you have an American style option, you can elect to purchase the underlying asset at any time before the contract expires. With a European style option, the holder cannot purchase an underlying security until the date of the contract expiration. If a holder buys an underlying asset, they are said to have exercised their option.

There are three different states that an options contract holder can experience: out of the money, in the money, and at the money. Out of the money is when the value of the asset is less than the strike price, in the money is when the underlying is worth more than the strike price, and at the money is when both the underlying asset and the strike price have an equal value.

Puts

Puts are basically the opposite of calls. The owner of a put purchases the right to sell an underlying asset at the strike price. A trader buys a put option when they expect the value of an underlying asset to decrease. The holder and the writer are the parties to a puts options contract. The person that purchases the contract is referred to as the holder, and they have the right to purchase the underlying asset at the strike price. Just as it happens with calls, puts can be based on a wide array of securities as well. Some of the common underlying assets that the contracts are based on include stocks, foreign currencies, indices, and commodities. You don't necessarily have to own the underlying asset physically at the time of put purchase. A naked put is when you don't own the underlying. Generally, puts are rarely exercised, and holders are usually in favor of monetary gain equal to the value of the underlying.

Puts can be classified into two broad classes: American style and European style. The American style put allows the holder to exercise the option at any time before or on the date of expiration of the contract. But under the terms of a European style put, the owner can only decide whether or not to exercise their option on the date of expiration. American style options might be expensive, but they are still popular because of the flexibility that they afford the owner.

American style

The term "American style" has no relation to America. It is merely a term for explaining the options contracts. The owner of an options contract will have to either purchase or sell the underlying asset either before the contract expires or at the date of expiration of the contract. The American style options allow the owner to exercise their option at any time before the contract expires.

European style

The owner of a European style option doesn't enjoy the flexibility of an American style option. Under the terms of a European style option, the owner of an options contract can exercise only on the expiration date of the contract.

Exchange-traded options

Listed options is the other name for exchange-traded options. It describes any options contracts that are listed on a public trading exchange. Any trader can purchase or sell the exchange-traded options through a broker.

Over the counter options

These are only ever traded in the over the counter markets, and the general public can hardly access them.

Option type by underlying asset

The most common form of underlying assets that the majority of options contracts are based on are the shares of a publicly listed company. But an underlying asset can take other varied forms, such as the following.

- **Index options:** These have a close similarity to stock options, except that the index, not the shares, is what the options are based on.

- **Forex/Currency options:** Contracts of this nature give the owner the authority to purchase or sell off a certain currency at an agreed rate of exchange.

- **Futures options:** The specified futures contract is the underlying security. A futures option allows the owner to enter into a specific futures contract.

- **Commodity options:** For a contract of this type, the underlying asset can be either a physical commodity or a commodity futures contract.

- **Basket options:** The underlying asset could be comprised of a group of securities, such as currencies, stocks, commodities, and other financial securities.

Option type by expiration

Contracts can be categorized by their cycle of expiration. Some contracts have a fixed cycle while others are a bit more flexible. Below are some of the contract types.

- **Regular options:** These are based on standard expiration cycles that contracts are listed under.

- **Weekly options:** They are similar to regular options but have a shorter period of expiration.

- **Quarterly options:** They are listed on exchanges with expirations for the nearest four quarters plus the following year's final quarter.

- **Long-term expiration anticipation securities (LEAPS):** These expire in January, but they can be purchased with the expiration dates for the next three years.

Employee stock options

An options contract can be based on the stock of the company that a person works for.

Exotic options

These are contracts that are customized with more sophisticated provisions. They are also known as non-standardized options. Following are some of the common types of exotic options:

- **Barrier options**
- **Binary options**
- **Chooser options**
- **Compound options**
- **Look back options**

Chapter 7

Options Prices and Valuation

Before you start trading options, you should first ensure that you have a deep comprehension of the aspects that impact an option's value. Some of the factors include the price of stock, time value, intrinsic value, volatility, cash dividends, and interest rates.

There are various models of pricing that utilize these measures to work out the option's market value. One of the most popular models is the Black-Scholes model. In order to make profits off of options trading, you have to understand what determines their prices and profit from the market moves.

What are the main influences of the price of an option?

The basic influences of an option's price are volatility, time value, intrinsic value, and market price. As the stock price oscillates up and down, it affects the option's price. When the price of stock moves up, the price of the call will be driven up as well, and the cost of the put will decrease. If the worth of the stock deteriorates, the price of the call suffers, and the put's price will go up.

Intrinsic value

The intrinsic value is the current worth of an option, i.e., how valuable it would be if it were exercised today. In other words, it is the figure by which an option's strike price is in the money (ITM). Intrinsic value is a friend of time. If the owner of an option exercised their option, the intrinsic value should help him earn a profit. For instance, let's say that the stocks of a company X are selling at $35 per share. The company X's $30 call option intrinsic value would be $5 ($35 – $30). The option holder can exercise his option to purchase the stocks of company X at $30 and then sell them off at $35, making a $5 profit.

The intrinsic value of calls is worked out by subtracting an underlying's price from the strike price, and the intrinsic value of puts is worked out by subtracting the strike price from the underlying's price. In both put options and call options, if the calculated value is negative, then the option has no intrinsic value. An option's total value is worked out by combining the intrinsic value and the time value. Time value takes into consideration external aspects that affect the price of an option.

Time value

An option's time value is the amount by which the price of an option tops the intrinsic value. It is connected to the remaining amount of time before the contract expires as well as to the stock price's volatility. This is the formula of working out the time value of an option:

Option Price – Intrinsic Value = Time Value

The more time there is before an option contract expires, the greater the possibility that it will end up ITM. An option's time component decays rapidly. The precise derivation of an option's time value is a fairly complex equation. Generally, an option loses a third of its value in the first half of its life and two-thirds in the second half of its life. The closer you are to the expiration of an options contract, the more that a move in the underlying asset is needed to impact the price of an option.

Basically, time value is worked out by subtracting the difference between the strike price and the underlying's price from the cost of the option. The more time there is before a contract expires, the higher time value the option enjoys and, thus, the higher the premium.

In the money

In the money means that the market price of the underlying is much greater than the strike price of a call option, or that the market price of an underlying is much less than the put's strike price. There's intrinsic value in an ITM option, but there's zero intrinsic value in an out of the money (OTM) option. An in the money option could allow the trader to earn a profit by exercising the option.

For instance, if Janet purchases a call for company Y's stock with a $12 strike price, and the stock price is $15, that option is in the money. Janet is entitled to buy the security for $12 and then turn around and sell it off at $15, thus making a profit of $3 per share.

At the money

At the money (ATM) is a situation in which both the values of an option and the strike are equal. Calls and puts can both be ATM. For instance, if the price of the shares of company Y is $75, then company Y 75 call option and company Y 75 put option are both at the money. There's no intrinsic value in ATM options.

Out of the money

Out of the money describes a call in which the value of the underlying is much less than the strike price, or a put in which the value of the underlying is much more than the strike price. An OTM option doesn't have any intrinsic value, but it could possess a time value.

Chapter 8

Roles of Options Exchanges

The options exchanges play a critical role in ensuring that there are enough securities to base options contracts on. Following are some of the significant functions of an options exchange.

Liquidity

Perhaps the biggest function of options exchanges is to ensure ready markets for options contracts. The markets ensure that holders of options can exercise their options and that there are enough buyers to purchase the options. Traders are looking for avenues to increase their earning potential, and liquidity helps them achieve that. Options contracts have a time limit unlike other securities such as shares, which necessitates liquidity. The existence of market makers is particularly responsible for liquidity.

Gauging a country's economy

The state of an options market can reliably inform us what the country's economic situation is like. The most common underlying assets that traders base their options on are shares. The prevailing economic conditions are always reflected in the share prices of various companies. If the country is experiencing prosperity, the share prices will be up, and if the country is experiencing market crashes, the share prices will go down. Thus, the options exchanges play a critical role in ensuring that traders have a sense of how their country is performing economy-wise. Stocks are the pulse of an economy, and they are accurate predictors of a country's economic state.

Securities pricing

Options traders have a wide pool to choose from when it comes to underlying assets. However, the value of an underlying asset is determined by the options exchange according to the forces of demand and supply. The financial securities of prosperous companies are worth more than the securities of moderately successful companies. The valuation of securities is important not only for traders but also for governments. Governments levy taxes on earnings drawn from options trading, so they first have to get the value of the securities.

Safety of transactions

Traders want to be sure that they can trust all the parties that they are getting into business with. Therefore, it is the work of an options exchange to ensure the players are trustworthy. For one, most options contracts are based on financial securities of publicly listed companies, and these companies must operate within stringent rules and regulations. Thus, the trader is assured of security when dealing with other parties. The options markets should provide all relevant information about options contracts and securities to discourage the trader from making a move out of ignorance.

Providing speculation scope

Speculation of securities is critical in order to ensure a healthy balance of demand and supply of securities. Many traders earn their profits from purely speculative risk. They have developed a skill of determining the movement of prices. The options exchanges provide traders with the resources and tools of speculating on the securities performance, thus allowing traders to earn profits.

Promotes investment culture

Options exchanges are critical in promoting the culture of investing in valuable securities like stock as opposed to unproductive assets such as precious metals. Traders have a wide selection of underlying securities to base their options contracts on; thus, they are not limited in the range of their strategies. A strong saving and investment culture is critical for the economic advancement of a country.

Continuous market for securities

Options exchanges allow traders to base their options on a wide range of underlying securities, and in case of any risks, traders are at liberty to switch from one security to the next. This is different from purchasing stocks wherein you are stuck with the consequences of poor decisions.

Capital formation

Options exchanges promote the pooling together and redistribution of resources. The exchanges create a win-win situation for both sides. Companies raise capital when their stocks are publicly listed, and their securities act as the underlying. On the other hand, traders stand to benefit from the high earning potential and low-capital requirements for options contracts. So, options exchanges play a critical role in ensuring that the parties are in a position to generate capital.

Control companies

The importance of transparency in the derivatives market cannot be overstated. If a trader has the misfortune of working with shady companies, they could easily lose their earnings. Options exchanges make it hard for shady companies to spoil the market. For instance, publicly traded companies have to submit relevant documents and adhere to certain performance standards as doing so will boost investor confidence. Companies that refuse to cooperate with exchanges are blacklisted from the market.

Fiscal and monetary policies

The fiscal policy and the monetary policy of the government must not hurt the players in the financial industry. Options exchanges facilitate the creation and execution of key policies that will govern the financial markets.

Proper canalization of wealth

Options are a great way of putting capital into great use, as opposed to having the capital just sitting around. Thus, the economy benefits from an injection of capital which would otherwise have been inactive. The injection of capital into the economy promotes wealth distribution and fights off economic disgraces like unemployment.

Education purposes

Options trading features complex processes. Even people who claim to understand options trading might be low-key deluded. Thus, the importance of education cannot be overstated. Many traders just get the hang of things and set about purchasing and selling options contracts, forgetting that it is critical to first educate one's self. Options exchanges provide a wealth of resources and information that are meant to enlighten traders. Empowered traders improve the trading activity.

Chapter 9

Roles of the Options Clearing Corporation

The Options Clearing Corporation (OCC) is the planet's largest firm that provides services in clearing, risk management, market intelligence, and settlement. Here are the critical roles that the OCC plays:

Clearing services
In the beginning, the Options Clearing Corporation was a clearinghouse only for listed equity options. The marketplace evolved, however, and now the OCC is a global clearinghouse for diverse and sophisticated financial securities. The OCC functions under the

jurisdiction of both the Commodities Futures Trading Commission (CFTC) and the SEC. Operating under the SEC jurisdiction, the OCC clears transactions for calls and puts on shares, foreign currencies, stock indexes, interest rates composites, single stock futures, and over the counter (OTC) options. Operating under the CFTC jurisdiction, the OCC delivers clearing services for transactions in options, covering stock indexes, interest rates, FX, volatile assets, and single stock. Additionally, the OCC offers central counterparty clearing and settlement services for transactions revolving around securities lending. The OCC has been christened as a systematic financial markets utility in the constitution.

By offering world-class clearing services for options, OTC, and other derivatives marketplaces, the OCC protects the integrity of the financial markets. In its role as the main counterparty and guarantor, the OCC ensures that the contract obligations are met. Operating through a novation process, the OCC both sells and buys, thus shielding its members from counterparty risk.

Since its establishment in the 1970s, the OCC has been dedicated to promoting financial integrity and stability in marketplaces by providing sound risk management principles, margin requirements, membership standards, and clearing fund. The services of OCC improve on the fulfillment of margin and settlement obligations while also promoting efficiency in back-office operations.

The OCC technical certification services are aimed at external business parties such as banks and trade sources. The services include the onboarding of new external parties. Some of the testing services provided are as follows.

- Processing verification and new transaction format
- Full-circle processing through real-time data transmission for
    - Options and futures

- Stock loan
- Delta position limit
- LOPR
- SOSA
- Collateral
- Creation of outputs and core reports

Market data

The OCC also gathers all the data relevant to the markets of its companies. The information is accurate, and it helps in making decisions that particularly touch on investment opportunities and strategies.

The OCC provides data on the volume and open interest of options and futures in the following formats:

- Volume query
- OTC open interest
- Daily volume
- Daily volume by exchange
- Futures open interest
- Put/call ratio
- Exchange volume by class
- Historical volume
- Daily open interest

Risk management

The OCC offers risk management services that include an organization's ability to withstand risk exposure. As the financial derivatives market expands throughout the world, the counterparty credit risk is high; hence, the need to analyze companies' capacity to thrive despite the risk involved. Through data analysis and numerical simulations, the OCC can weigh a company's ability to withstand risk exposure.

Through the STANS methodology, the OCC can measure the level of risk exposure of options and futures portfolios. The STANS methodology facilitates measuring, monitoring, and managing the level of risk of the OCC members' portfolios. A clearinghouse offers transparency and reduces systemic risk. The OCC maintains the integrity of the market and protects capital by standing in the middle of each transaction, acting as the central counterparty.

The OCC implements a model of managing risk that will protect its members and the larger markets from defaults. Some of the methods that the OCC employs in managing risk include the following:

- **Stringent membership standards.** The benefits of acquiring OCC membership include
    - Real-time ENCORE clearing technology, thanks to state-of-the-art technology;
    - Financial guarantee;
    - Utility model that promotes low transaction fees;
    - Central processing;
    - Cross-margin;
    - Fungibility;

- Direct access to reports;
- World-class customer services.

But in order to enjoy all these benefits, you have to meet their high standards. These are the requirements for applying to become a member:

- You must be a dealer or FCM with an SEC or a CFTC registration.
- You must meet the minimum net capital conditions.
- Your staff must be qualified, and you should have the capacity to self-clear options and interface with the OCC.
- You must submit a complete form through the OCC's online gateway.
- You must submit all the relevant paperwork.
- You must submit audited financial statements.
- You must provide the findings of commodities and securities regulators.
- You must pay a non-refundable fee.

The high standards of membership ensure that the OCC will have the capacity to answer to its members' needs.

- **Continuous position monitoring.** The OCC monitors positions and margins throughout the day to manage the clearing risk. If the OCC neglected this responsibility, critical issues might pop up and have a compounding effect, culminating in a crisis.

- **Intraday mark-to-market margining.** The OCC reevaluates cleared portfolios on a regular basis and requires members to pay their losses in order to discourage its compounding. Clearing members who have losing positions are held to account.

- **Margin calls.** The OCC reserves the right to make intraday margin calls as it deems appropriate.

- **Default resources.** Some members do default, and in that case, the OCC will step in to resolve the issue. It keeps a substantial fund reserve that caters to member defaults.

- **Rigorous stress testing.** The OCC simulates various market scenarios in order to improve accuracy and to sufficiently minimize risk and promote market integrity.

- **Transparency.** This is one of the essential qualities in a clearinghouse. The OCC provides comprehensive documentation on the rules, risks, obligations, and fees. In this way, the member is fully aware of the terms of agreement with the OCC.

- **Independent committee.** The OCC has an independent team that keeps watch over the financial markets and maintains oversight of the activities of the OCC in order to ensure that appropriate risk mitigation steps are always taken.

Chapter 10

How to Open a Trading Account

Trading in the financial derivatives market has a high earning potential, but you'll require tools for the research and execution of each trade. In order to trade options, you will have to work with an options broker. In the past, opening a trading account was a resource-intensive undertaking considering how the average broker had many clients. However, since the advent of the internet, it has become quite convenient to open an options trading account both in terms of time and money. Online trading accounts guarantee immediacy and small fees.

Scout for options brokers

You have to select the trading platform that suits your needs best. As a beginner, the best options broker is the one that offers extensive educational resources and is responsive to your needs. Some of the most reputable online options brokers include Fidelity, E*Trade, Interactive Brokers, and TD Ameritrade. Here are some guidelines for selecting the best options broker:

- **Compare fees.** There are many options brokers, and they charge differently. Take your time to scout for the options broker whose fees you feel comfortable paying. The more you research, the more you will increase your prospects.

- **Check the reviews.** Thanks to the internet, you can now judge the viability of an options broker based on other peoples' experience. There are many websites dedicated to rating options brokers, wherein past users of the brokerages will leave either a positive or a negative review. Check to see whether the brokerage is listed as a scam site as they will steal your money. Judging from the reviews, you can make a decision as to which options broker would be the best pick for you.

- **Documents.** Find out which documents your options broker will want to get from you.

- **Minimum deposit.** Check the minimum deposit and decide whether or not you can afford it. Depending on the level of traders they handle, various options brokers will have different minimums.

- **Payment.** Check the payment methods of your chosen brokerage to see whether you're prepared. Most of their payments are processed by secure platforms such as PayPal, Payoneer, and Skrill.

Application

The application process is quite easy and fast, as you're only required to fill out an online form and submit with the click of a button. Depending on the broker, your account might be activated immediately, or they might have to review your application first before activating your account.

Approval

Your options broker reserves the right to give the approval before you could trade options. They can impose limits on your account based on your trading expertise and the amount you deposited. Brokers have the responsibility of ensuring that you understand the level of risk you're subjecting yourself to.

Technical analysis

Technical analysis will assist you with predicting the future performance of various tradable assets. If you develop your skills in this aspect, you'll be well on your way into reaping huge profits. However, you must understand that the predictions are not unequivocal. There's no surefire way of determining how financial securities will perform in the future. When you commit your resources into buying options contracts, always subject yourself to the level of risk that you can handle.

Chapter 11

Placing Your Order

Placing your first order is not as difficult as many newbie traders seem to think. All you have to do is obtain the right information and apply yourself. Following are the steps for placing your first order:

- o **Login to your brokerage account.** When you sign up for the services of an online broker, you will be issued a username and password. These are the credentials that will enable you to log in to your account. You must keep them secret. In fact, you should even add more security features to keep your account fail-safe. There are many degrees of fraudulent activities on the internet, but protecting yourself against these frauds starts with securing your account.

- **Find the trade or order page.** It depends on the user interface of various platforms, but since you have opened a trading account, there must be an item on the page labeled "trade" or "order." Brokerages invest in a simple interface so that traders could interact with the options exchange quite easily.

- **Pull up a stock or ETF quote.** Stocks are the commonest underlying securities that options are based on, so you have to pull the quotes of the company shares that you're targeting.

- **Search for the options quote table.** Next up, you have to check the underlying and options price, which are placed conveniently on the search results.

- **Choose your expiration date.** Unlike shares, options have time constraints, so next, you have to select the frame of time within which you will trade, which requires you to set the expiration date of your options contract.

- **Select your strike price.** The strike prices for both put options and call options are clearly shown in the table, and you have to select the strike price that you want.

- **Select either "call" or "put."** The calls are typically listed on the left side of the page while the puts are listed on the right side. Select the option that you want and check the quotes. The order form for the option will come up.

- **Enter the quantity.** Now you have to enter the number of contracts that you wish to purchase. But remember that as a beginner, you have to be careful, which means you have to purchase a relatively small amount of options contracts before you dive all the way in.

- **Set your desired price.** Set the price at which you'll acquire the options contract. The premium is influenced by many aspects, among them, the stock price of the underlying.

- **Choose the order type.** This is an advanced feature that can help you manage the risk to an extent.

- **Day order or GTC order.** At this point, you will decide how long the order will stay open if it's not filled. Day orders stay open during the day and automatically turn off at the close of the market. GTC orders refer to "Good Till Canceled Orders," which means they will stay open until they are either filled or canceled.

- **Confirm and send.** At the click of a button, your order is placed. Don't rush to do it. Take a moment to review your order so as to ensure that there are no errors.

Chapter 12

What Are Options Chains?

Many online brokerages present the information that investors are interested in in the form of a table. Depending on the financial instrument, or the broker in question, the design and format of the table will vary. For instance, tables that show futures have a different design than tables that show stocks.

A table that an options broker uses to display information concerning options contracts is known as an option chain. Some options chains can be basic, whereas others can contain intricate details. Traders may study one type of chain or many different types, depending on the information that they are looking for or the nature of the trades they intend to execute.

The three commonly used options chains formats are as follows:

- Basic options chain
- Options pricer
- Options strategy chain

Basic options chain

Newbie traders find the basic options chain very useful. It promotes a straightforward trading strategy of buying either call options or put options with the intention of selling them off at a profit. The basic options chain displays in one page the puts and calls related to the same underlying, except that the strike prices are dissimilar. The basic options chain has a number of columns, and each column shows information relating to the listed contract. Typically, the put options are on the right side of the page while the call options are on the left side. The information contained in the columns of most basic options chains include the following.

- **Options symbol:** This signifies the identity of the option. It indicates the underlying security, the month of expiration, and the strike price.

- **Expiration date:** For purposes of classification, contracts with a similar expiration date are shown on the same page.

- **Strike price:** This is usually displayed in the middle column of a basic options chain. Put options and call options that have the same strike price are shown on the same row.

- **Bid price:** Indicates at what price you can sell the contract.

- o **Ask price:** Indicates at what price you can purchase the contract.

- o **Last price:** Indicates the price at which the contract was last transacted.

- o **Volume:** Indicates the amount of the sales and purchase of the option during the trading day.

- o **Open interest:** Indicates the options that have been written but are yet to expire, exercised, or bought back by the writer.

Options pricer

The options pricer assists the investor with understanding how market conditions influence the price of the option that they're considering to trade. Options pricer contains similar information as the basic options chain, and the only additions are the five options in Greek letters, i.e., Delta, Gamma, Theta, Vega, and Rho. Options pricers typically display only put options or only call options on the screen, meaning that you have to switch between tables to compare prices. They are user-friendly, and you can adjust certain variables for convenience.

Options strategy chain

Advanced traders find the options strategy chain to be the most useful options chain. They involve combining standardized strategies into a single position. Options strategy chain makes a number of complex calculations for the trader and displays useful data.

Chapter 13

How to Make Trades

When you purchase an options contract, you gain the right to either purchase or sell off the underlying. For instance, if the underlying of your options is shares, you gain the authority to buy 100 shares per contract at a strike price before or on a specific date. Making a trade involves three strategic choices:

- Decide the direction that the underlying is going to move
- Predict the changes in stock prices—whether high or low
- Predict the timeframe during which the underlying will move

Decide which direction you think the stock is going to move

This is what determines the type of options that you will select. If you think that the underlying's value will climb up, you purchase a call option contract. The call option will entitle you to purchase the underlying at the strike price within a specified timeframe.

If you are of the mind that the stock price will go down, you purchase a put option. A put option entitles you, but not obligates you, to sell off the underlying before the expiry date at the strike price.

Predict the changes in stock price—whether high or low

An option is only valuable if, at the close of the option, the underlying is in the money. This means that the trader would earn a profit if they exercise their option. For instance, if you predict that the share price of company X will rise from $100 to $120, you will buy a call with a strike price below $120. If the share price surpasses the strike price, your option becomes profitable.

If you predict that the share price of the same company X is going to fall from $100 to $80, you will buy a put whose strike price moves beyond the $80 mark so that the option remains profitable even at $80. If the strike price is greater than the underlying, the option is in the money.

The premium is the sum that you pay to acquire the options contract, and it typically comprises time value and intrinsic value. An option's intrinsic value is worked out by subtracting the value of the underlying's from the strike price of the option. Time value is the premium that has surpassed the option's intrinsic value.

Predict the timeframe during which the underlying will move

You can exercise the option before the expiration of the contract or on the day the contract expires. Your choice of the date of expiration is limited to what is made available on the option chain. The more time an option will take to expire, the higher its premium; the less time it will take to expire, the lesser the premium.

Here are some of the crucial guidelines that help traders to maximize their earning potential and at the same time limit their risk:

- Always have a trading plan
- Approach trading like a business and not a hobby
- Utilize technology
- Shield your trading capital against any unnecessary risk
- Study the derivatives market
- Risk only what you can afford to lose
- Develop a sound trading methodology centered on facts and not emotions
- Limit your exposure to risk with a Stop Loss
- If your trading plan is consistently unproductive, stop trading and sharpen your skills
- Have an objective and stay true to your goal

Chapter 14

Significant Trading Tools

These tools are not only incredibly useful but also free of charge!

Demo account

Not all brokerages provide demo accounts, but there's nothing that boosts a trader's confidence and morale more than executing trades on a demo account, just to get the hang of trading. Demo accounts are designed in a manner that simulates real trading platforms. They come loaded with virtual funds, assets, tools, and various option types. A newbie trader has the chance of testing their strategies without the risk of losing their money. Even experienced traders can simulate new trade strategies and carry out analysis and use the findings to maximize their earning potential. Most demo accounts have time limits, though. A trader must make the best use of a demo account while they still have time.

Trading bots

Thanks to the advancement in technology and particularly in artificial intelligence, a trader can automate their account. There are successful options traders who seem to trade only with bots. The effectiveness of a trading bot will depend on the manufacturer and on whether it's free or paid. Paid bots appear to achieve remarkable results as compared to free bots. They have robust systems that make it easy to predict the movement of various financial securities. However, they don't guarantee profits. It is up to you to figure out when to deploy bots and when to trade in person.

OptionsOracle

The OptionsOracle is one of the most comprehensive tools that assist traders in maximizing their profits. This tool helps traders visualize options strategies. The tool facilitates the analysis of stock options trading strategies. The tool favors even beginner-level traders. It is easy to use, and its interface is customizable. The default data feed of OptionsOracle is Yahoo Finance, although you can integrate your brokerage live data. Some of its key features include the following:

- Portfolio manager
- Options Greek calculator
- Options pain analysis
- Strategy analysis
- Volatility smile graph

StockFetcher

This is a free interactive chart that helps traders improve their accuracy in predicting the movement of the underlying. The chart features stock screens and machine intelligence that match stocks based on previous configurations. The tool allows you to build custom stock screens based on filters that are supported by more than 125 indicators. This web-based tool covers many sectors, and some of its features are as follows:

- Filter editor
- My filters
- Watch lists
- Chart+
- Shared lists
- Reports

Chapter 15

Strategies for Options Trading

One of the biggest mistakes that traders make is to jump into options trading without understanding the options strategies at their disposal to limit risk and maximize profits. Traders should apply themselves a bit more in order to take advantage of the flexibility and power of options trading. Here are some critical option strategies:

Covered call

Apart from buying a naked call option, you can also buy basic buy-write strategy or covered call. This strategy allows you to buy the assets right away and simultaneously write a call option on the exact same assets. Traders tend to favor this position when they have a short-term position and a neutral view of the asset and when they are looking to make more profits or hedge against a potential decline in the worth of the underlying. The covered call strategies are particularly useful in flat markets. A long position and a short call option are paired together on the same security. When the two positions are combined, the results can be higher returns and lower volatility.

Married put

In a married put strategy, an investor who buys a particular asset at the same time buys a put option for an equal amount of shares. Most investors practice the married put when they are bullish on the asset price and would like to shield themselves against loss in the short term. This strategy promotes security should the price of the asset fall down. When the value of the underlying falls, the value of the put of that stock is driven up. Married puts denote two different purchases, i.e., stock option and put option. A married put should be viewed as insurance as opposed to an opportunity to cash in. That is, you expect the stock price to go up, but you also have protective measures in place should your stock dive down.

Bull call spread

In a bull call spread strategy, a trader will concurrently purchase calls at a certain strike price and sell them at a greater strike price; the two call options share a common expiration date and underlying asset. The simultaneous purchase and selling of two different strikes leave an outlay of cash after buying one side of the spread and a simultaneous receipt of option premium when trading the other side. The basic credit spreads have an equal combination. The simultaneous purchase and trading of options with different strike prices create a spread position. A net credit occurs when the sold option is more expensive than the bought option.

Bear put spread

The bear put spread strategy mimics the bull call spread strategy. In this situation, the trader concurrently buys puts at a certain strike price and then sells off the puts at a lower strike price. Both options share the same underlying and expiry. This method is mostly applied when the trader is bearish and anticipates the underlying to depreciate. For instance, let's say that you purchase a put with a $50 strike price and the stock trades at $51 per share. The expiration date is 60 days away, and there's $2.50 strike price. A trader would have to pay $250 as premium, and before the contract expires, they would be at liberty to sell 100 stocks of the underlying at the price of $100 per share. In the event that the stock price falls, the holder could sell the stock. The trader could then purchase that exact same stock at the current price and pocket whatever is left.

Protective collar

A protective collar strategy is realized by buying an out of the money put while at the same time writing an out of the money call for the same security. The purpose of the protective collar strategy is to shield traders against losses and to allow them to maximize their earning potential when the markets go up. A protective collar is made up of a put option and a call option, which is basically a covered call and a long put position. Both the put and call are characteristically out of the money options, yet they share the same expiration date. The short call and long put merge together to form a "collar" for the underlying stock.

Long straddle

A long straddle options strategy refers to a situation whereby a trader simultaneously buys both a call and put option with similar underlying asset, strike price, and date of expiration. The long straddle strategy is typically implemented when a trader believes that an underlying asset will jump but is unsure about which side. The strategy is aimed at ensuring that the trader maintains unlimited gains, and the only losses that might be incurred are the premiums of the options contracts. There are two types of straddles:

- **Long straddle:** This strategy is great for buying a call and a put that share both the strike price and the expiration date. The long straddle especially takes advantage of the changes in market price.

- **Short straddle:** The short straddle strategy refers to when a trader sells a put and a call option on the same expiry date. The holder sells off the options and pockets the premium as profit.

Butterfly spread

In this strategy, a trader merges together the bear spread and the bull spread and uses different strike prices.

Iron condor

The iron condor strategy involves the trader concurrently holding two positions in varying strategies.

Iron butterfly

This is where a trader combines a long or short straddle with their simultaneous sale or purchase. The iron butterfly bears similarities to a butterfly spread, the difference being that both calls and puts are used as opposed to one or the other.

Chapter 16

Sources of Information

One of the things that professional traders cannot get enough of is information. There's a constant demand for relevant information touching upon financial securities. Traders want to evaluate the performance of various assets in the financial markets so that they can carefully select their underlying assets. An enlightened trader is more likely to maximize their earnings than an ignorant trader. So here are some of the sources of relevant financial markets information:

Consolidated tapes

A consolidated tape is an electronic system that conveys the latest data on exchange-listed shares. Consolidated tapes utilize advanced technology to report shares prices and sales volume that almost mimic real-time reporting. In the options markets, price oscillation is a common thing. The price of an underlying could move up and down within the space of hours or even minutes. Therefore, a trader who intends to keep a hawk's eye view of the trading activity ought to use a system that relays information quickly—i.e., consolidated tapes.

Consolidated tapes succeeded old ticker-tape machines that tracked exchange-traded stocks. The "Network A" covers the NYSE-listed securities, and it shows both the per share bid price of the latest traded block and the originating market. "Network B" shows Amex-listed securities and securities listed on local exchanges.

Pink Sheets

Pink Sheets is a private firm that caters to the over the counter securities markets. This private firm provides prices, quotations, and related information. Pink Sheets took its role of being a gateway of information in 1904 when the National Quotation Bureau began as a quotation service connecting rival market makers in the over the counter securities markets across the USA. Pink Sheets offers an online quotation service for the securities markets, and market makers, broker-dealers, and the public can access the portal.

Yellow Sheets

The Yellow Sheets is a daily bulletin provided by the National Quotation Bureau that shows bids and ask prices for over the counter-corporate bonds. The Yellow Sheets also showcases broker-dealers that act as market makers in those bonds.

Nasdaq

Auctions are carried out in the exchanges, and the stock price is determined by the investor who outbids everyone else. In OTC markets, stocks are traded on a negotiated basis. The owners of shares engage in offers and counter-offers known as bids and ask prices. The Nasdaq is the most famous part of the OTC markets. Nasdaq displays the largest equity securities market in the USA on state-of-the-art digital platforms.

Nasdaq provides information on a subscription basis. Subscribers are divided into three plans, and the information that each subscriber receives depends on the plan that they are subscribed to.

Before a company can be listed on Nasdaq, it has to meet various standards market capitalization, shareholders' equity, and per-share price. Not every publicly listed company can meet Nasdaq's requirements, and even then, not all companies that meet Nasdaq's requirements are interested in getting listed. The OTC market promotes the trading of low-share prices also known as "penny stock."

The Over the Counter Bulletin Board displays last-sale prices, real-time quotes, and volume data for over the counter securities not listed on Nasdaq. The securities listed on the Over the Counter Bulletin Board include stocks, ADRs, DPPs, and warrants. The assets are traded by a group of market makers connected together through a closed computer network.

Blue List

The Blue List is the best source of municipal and corporate bond information. It showcases municipal and corporate bond offerings, market reviews, income statistics, and other news touching on bonds. Their website provides a ticker service.

Bond Buyer

This publication provides news, statistics, data, and analysis touching upon the municipal bond market. Unlike the Blue List, the Bond Buyer centers its attention on municipal bonds alone.

Apps

The quickest way to access information is by using your phone. Software engineers in the FinTech industry have developed apps that allow options traders to stay up-to-date on market news and opportunities. These are some of the critical apps that every trader should download to their phone:

- **TradeStation Mobile:** This app enjoys a high rating across many review websites and is available for free to all the clients of TradeStation. TradeStation Mobile allows traders to look at a huge amount of options contracts with varying strike prices and dates of expiration. The app also allows traders to view options chains and charts with an assortment of technical indicators. Aside from supplying you with all the relevant market information, the TradeStation Mobile app comes with a trading account; thus, traders can make or cancel orders with a few clicks.

- **Stock Option Quotes:** This app offers options-related news and quotes. The app has a tool for tracking the performance of options in the US derivatives market. With just a click of a button, traders can access various call and put options with different strike prices and dates of expiration. The app also allows the trader to access options information concerning various financial securities listed on the regional exchanges. Stocks and indexes can be viewed through interactive charts, and the menu can be customized, allowing you to put the options listings you're interested in on top. All these functionalities can not only increase your awareness but also make trading more fruitful.

- **AZFinance app:** This app provides news and quotations for virtually every financial market. When you have this app on your phone, you will have access to the latest news pertaining to nearly every securities market that you're interested in. This can help you improve your trading strategies considering that options contracts can be based on a wide range of underlying securities.

Chapter 17

Common Mistakes to Be Wary of

The following are some of the pitfalls that options traders fall into, leading them to suffer losses.

Buying out of the money call options

Most options traders adhere to the strategy of buying low and selling high. However, when you buy out of the money calls, you hurt your chances of making a profit, and when the losing streak becomes prolonged, it could render your trading strategy unproductive. The ones who are most susceptible to this mistake are the traders who operate on a small budget.

Giving in to fear and greed

Options trading requires a trader to be very forward-thinking and in charge of their emotions. But traders don't always exercise their emotional intelligence. For instance, when a trade is winning, an investor might get greedy and resist closing their position, simply because they want to allow the trade more time to go even further up. Greed can also manifest when an options trader is adamant despite the fact that they are losing consistently. When losses become your constant companion, it's time to pull out and reevaluate your strategies. If you're executing appropriate trading strategies, there's no reason you should struggle to make a profit. Traders who are driven by fear tend to overreact to every small thing that goes wrong. For instance, they bail out at the first sign of incurring a loss.

Doing poor allocation

Never commit more than 5% of your portfolio to one options trade. In as much as options have leverage and high earning potential, you cannot ignore the high level of risk exposure. Thus, you have to allocate prudently.

Having a finite approach

Options are flexible and can work with almost any securities market. But a single trading strategy doesn't achieve the same results across all securities markets. If an underlying asset is hardly moving, an out of the money call or put option is likely to expire worthless. However, taking covered options can be profitable in this scenario. Iron Condor, a trading strategy that involves taking many positions, would generate a profit in the event that the underlying moves slowly.

Not having an exit plan

Before you start trading, you should fully understand what you're trying to get into. How much money do you intend to make? What are your risk-reduction measures? Once you have answered the critical questions, you will be in a position to make appropriate strategies and learn how to exit with the least possible scars when you're losing money.

Being oblivious to market moving events

Let's say you create an options trade based on a stagnant market. You make a profit even though the underlying market barely moves. In case of volatility, your strategy would be thrown into jeopardy. Thus, you have to stay abreast of what is happening in the market in order to spot investment opportunities. An options trader who stays complacent will never realize their full earning potential.

Ignoring consistent profits in favor of home runs

Options traders tend to forgo the chance of making small yet consistent amounts of profits and focus their energies on nailing the elusive home run. If you have a trading strategy that seems to net you small but consistent earnings, you should stick to that. Thanks to the power of compounding effect, the earnings will add up to an impressive amount over time.

Buying naked options without hedging

Naked options describe a situation where the writer doesn't own the underlying assets. When a trader takes this approach, they should have the sense to at least hedge. Naked options expose the writer to unlimited loss.

Trying to time legged trades

Options traders often take multiple options positions in the same instance. Several transactions are required for such trades, and they should all take place at the same time to achieve the desired positioning. Some traders will attempt to make the transactions separately, trying to increase their earnings by getting an option on the uptick and another on the downtick. If you miss the window to establish the position, you expose yourself to unlimited loss. When you create a position that requires several options trades, take them all at once instead of cherry picking your entry points.

Having a strategy that doesn't match your outlook

An options trader is supposed to have an outlook of what they expect to happen. Technical analysis and fundamental analysis play a part in developing your outlook. Technical analysis promotes the interpretation of the market's volume and price on a chart, whereas fundamental analysis is mostly about reviewing a company's performance data. Thus, a trader must always take the trading strategy that marries their outlook.

Choosing an inappropriate date of expiration

The date of expiration affects the price of an option. But due to incompetence and carelessness, many traders select dates of expiration that hurt their chances of making profits. An option must accommodate the aspect of timeframe. It becomes easier to select the timeframe when you have developed an outlook. Before you select the date of expiration, it is prudent to first ask yourself the following questions:

- How long will it take for the trade to be carried out?

- Should I hold the event via an earnings announcement or a stock split?

- Do I have adequate liquidity to support my trade?

Not using probability

You have to take into account the probabilities of your strategy before you place your trade. When you use probability, it puts your outlook into perspective and gives a structure to the risk/reward hurdle.

Not having a trading plan

You have to be quite smart in order to become a successful options trader. Instead of basing your investment decisions on emotions, you should come up with sound trading plans. Your trading plan is what informs the actions you will take with your options contracts. When drafting a trading plan, here are some of the important questions that should be answered:

- How much can you risk in a single trade?

- What are the opportunities in the financial markets?

- When will you enter the trade?

- What is your strategy for exiting?

Conclusion

Options are a type of derivative asset. The premium that you pay to acquire an options contract is influenced by a number of factors, such as the underlying's value and the prevailing market conditions. An options contract entitles the holder to buy or sell the underlying either before the contract expires or on the day that the contract expires. The strike price refers to the price that an underlying asset can be sold or bought. When the underlying's value goes above the strike price, the call option is in the money, and thus, the owner would make a profit if they exercised their option. The holders of options contracts are under no obligation to buy or sell. It is entirely up to them whether or not to exercise the option.

www.ingramcontent.com/pod-product-compliance
Lightning Source LLC
Chambersburg PA
CBHW052338220526
45472CB00001B/473